Ernest Rhys

A London Rose And Other Rhymes

Ernest Rhys

A London Rose And Other Rhymes

ISBN/EAN: 9783744692878

Printed in Europe, USA, Canada, Australia, Japan

Cover: Foto ©Thomas Meinert / pixelio.de

More available books at **www.hansebooks.com**

A LONDON ROSE

AND

OTHER RHYMES

A·LONDON·ROSE & OJHER·RHYMES

BY
E·RNESJ·RHYS

1894
LONDON
ELKIN MAJHEWS & IOHN LANE
NEW YORK·DODD MEAD AND C○

TO

THE DEARER DIANA

OF THESE DAYS

CONTENTS

CONTENTS

V. OCCASIONAL VERSE

I

A LONDON ROSE
AND OTHER
RHYMES

A LONDON ROSE

Diana, take this London rose,
  Of crimson grace for your pale hand,
Who love all loveliness that grows :
A London rose—ah, no one knows,
  A penny bought it in the Strand !

But not alone for heart's delight;
  The crimson has a deeper stain
For your kind eyes that, late by night,
Grew sad at London's motley sight
  Beneath the gaslit driving rain.

And now again I fear you start
  To find that sorry comedy
Re-written on a rose's heart :
'Tis yours alone to read apart,
  Who have such eyes to weep and see.

Soon rose and rhyme must die forgot,
  But this, Diana—ah, who knows !
May die, yet live on in your thought
Of London's fate, and his, who bought
  For love of you a London rose.

LONDON FEAST

O WHERE do you go, and what's your will,
My sunburnt herdsmen of the hill,
  That leave your herds no pastoral priest,
And take the road where, sad and dun,
The smoke-cloud drapes the April sun?—
          ' We go to taste
           Of London Feast.'

O country-lads, this April tide,
Why do you leave the country-side?
  The new-come Spring stirs bird and beast;
The winter storm is over now,
And melted the December snow :—
          ' We go to taste
           Of London Feast.'

O village maidens, April girls,
With dancing eyes and country curls,
  Is April nought, the Maypole ceased,
That you must leave the daisied places
That painted all your pretty faces?—
                          ' We go to taste
                            Of London Feast.'

And ancient dalesmen of the north,
That leave your dales, and the sweet brown earth,
  Are country acres so decreased,
And Cumbrian fells no longer ringing
With bleating lambs, and blackbirds singing?—
                          ' We go to taste
                            Of London Feast.'

O sailor lads, that love the sea,
Are you, too, of this company?—
  The shifting wind's no longer east;
Yet you have put the helm about,
To come ashore, and join the rout?—
                          ' We go to taste
                            Of London Feast.'

Too late, my golden mariners!
I have seen there these many years,
   How Most grew more, and less grew Least;
And now you go too late; the board
Cannot one crumb to you afford:

                 You cannot taste
                 Of London Feast.

Too late, dear children of the sun;
For London Feast is past and gone!
   I sat it out, and now released
Make westward from its weary gate.
Fools and unwise, you are too late:

                 You cannot taste
                 Of London Feast.

They did not heed, they would not stay;
I saw the dust on London way
   By denser thousands still increased:
My cry was vain. As they went by
Their murmur ran, for all reply:—

                 ‘ *We go to taste*
                 Of London Feast.’

A WINTER-NIGHT'S BACCHANTE

THE little tumult of the hour is past,
  The quick beseeching of the music, still,
    That made the moments reel,
While night gave way, and faster and more fast
Pressed tirelessly her circling feet upon romance's
    heel.

The spell was hers,—hers fiddle, piping flute,
  Whose rapturous magic sped the giddy throng,
    While swift she glanced along,
A pale Bacchante, passionate of foot,
Whose swaying limbs and laughing eyes turned all
    our hearts to song.

She charmed the night till care was stolen away,
  And left us happy, for an hour of heaven,
    Our sins of earth forgiven,
As still we watched white arms, white garments,
    sway,
And radiantly she swept along, by winds of music
    driven.

Now dawn is wintry in the sleeping street,
    And day comes back to cast its gloom on men,—
    Ah me !   I think, and then,
I see white garments sway, and circling feet,
That charm the wintry gloom away, and bring
      delight again.

But she is gone ; and only now in dreams
    May fancy follow, over land and sea,
    To where her haunt may be,
Where in the lyric south her footing seems
As of the fawn that wakes the day in fabled
      Italy.

ON A HARP

PLAYING IN A LONDON FOG

WHAT Ariel, far astray, with silver wing,
  Upborne with airy music, silver-sweet,
    Haunts here the London street?—
And from the fog, with harping string on
    string,
  Laughs in the ear, and spurs the lagging feet,
While Caliban-like, London sulks, though all the
    stars should sing.

Such mystic harping once its silvery scale
  Ran in grey Harlech, and on Merlin's Hill,
    Where listening fancy still
Can hear it, like some song in fairy-tale ;
  And still in Broceliaunde the oak-trees will
Repeat its lingering sighing strain to many a cold
    sea-vale.

Here harps the mystic noise should make the
   dead
   Of London wake, and all its walls have ears ;
      As when in Troy the spears
Rang in the streets, by Helen's beauty sped :
   Here harps the song of Merlin, or the spheres :
But London sleeps, unmoved, and dreams his other
   dreams instead.

So may he sleep,—the waking hour unknown,
   When Ariel's song shall end what it began,
      And waken Caliban.
And yet, who knows, his sleep is lighter grown
   By half-a-song's weight, since that chiming ran,
Athwart the fog, like thistledown o'er misty up-
   lands blown.

WESTMINSTER

THE play is done, and shadow lies,
Where late the empire of an hour
Waxed great and waned before men's eyes;
And homeward I, with brooding thought
Of art that bravely comes to flower,
                    And soon is nought.

I dream of art, remembering well
The hopes it gave, that still up-soared,
But one by one defeated fell,
Cast out eternally from heaven,
Like those lost angels that their Lord
                    From grace had driven.

So moved, to royal Westminster
Betimes I come, and gladly find
Those stately churches towering there,
Whose walls that Milton saw, we see :
Ah were, I cried, like these my mind !
                    Great praise might be.

Were strength like theirs that hold the night
With solemn watch, though London sleep,
To arm my soul with steadfast might,
Then fear might end and hope be sure.
Could I like them my vigil keep,
            Like them endure.

But they were built 'twixt hope and fear
By men who took the passing day,
And gave its moments heavenly wear;
Though they who built are darkly gone
Their art remains, and in it they
            Are greatly known.

So art is frail, but art is strong;
And he is wise who keeps the way
His soul shall lead, and sings his song,
Or bids dead stone take life and climb,—
So yields his service for a day,
            Or for all time.

CHATTERTON IN HOLBORN

From country fields I came, that hid
  The harvest mice at play,
And followed care, whose summons bid
  To London's troubled way.

And there, in wandering far and wide,
  I chanced ere day was done
Where Holborn poured its civic tide
  Beneath the autumn sun.

So hot the sun, so great the throng,
  I gladly stayed my feet
To hear a linnet's captive song
  Accuse the noisy street.

There heavily an old house bowed
  Its gabled head, and made
Obeisance to the modern crowd
  That swept athwart its shade.

Below, an open window kept
  Old books in rare display,
Where critics drowsed and poets slept
  Till Grub Street's judgment-day.

One book brought care again to me,—
    The book of Rowley's rhyme,
That Chatterton, in seigneury
    Of song, bore out of time.

The merchant of such ware, unseen,
    Watched spider-like the street;
He came forth, grey, and spider-thin,
    And talked with grave conceit.

Old books, old times,—he drew them nigh
    At Chatterton's pale spell:
''Twas Brook Street,' said he, 'saw him die,
    Old Holborn knew him well.'

The words brought back in sudden sway
    That new-old tale of doom;
It seemed the boy but yesterday
    Died in his lonely room.

Without, the press of men was heard;
    I heard, as one who dreamed,
The hurrying throng, the singing bird,
    And yesterday it seemed.

And as I turned to go, the tale
    A pensive requiem made,
As though within the churchyard rail
    The boy was newly laid:

REQUIEM

' Perhaps, who knows ? the hurrying throng
  Gave hopeless thoughts to him ;
I fancy how he wandered, long,
  Until the light grew dim.

' The windows saw him come and pass
  And come and go again,
And still the throng swept by—alas !
  The barren face of men.

' And when the day was gone, the way
  Led down the lethal deeps :
Sweet Life ! what requiem to say ?—
  'Tis well, 'tis well, he sleeps ! '

ORANGE SONG

TO BRIAN AND MARGARET, WITH SOME SICILIAN ORANGES

CHILDREN, these gold orbs were won
From the circling of the sun,
Where its golden light is free
On the shores of Sicily.
Northward, then the ship set sail,
Brought them here to tell the tale,—
Brought them by the bold sea-way,
Round to London's wintry day.

Now, their sweetness of the south,
Quartered, kiss each merry mouth !
And their fragrances be spent
On the air in sweeter scent.
But ere yet you all unseal them
Of their sweets, and lightly peal them
Of their yellow jackets,—stay !
Ere you taste, in golden play
Spin them, children, in the sight
Of the friendly red firelight;

And their golden wayward dancing,
Over wall and ceiling glancing,
Shall like fairy suns illume
All the deep December gloom.

They shall still go shining on
Then, and still your eyes be feasted ;
They shall be in fancy tasted
Then, when all their gold is gone.

IN A LONDON CHAMBER

STRANGE things pass nightly in this little room,
    All dreary as it looks by light of day ;
    Enchantment reigns here when at evening play
Red firelit glimpses through the pallid gloom :
Then come—perchance the shadows there assume
    The guise—heroic guests in dim array,
    The kings of eld, returned the human way
By Bridge of Dread, from star to straitening tomb.

High dreams they bring that never were dreamt in
      sleep :
    These walls yawn wide to Time and Death and
      Hell,
    To the last abyss of men's wild cries to Heaven ;
While night uncurtains on a sobbing deep,
    And lo ! the land wherein the Holy Grail,
    In far Monsalvat to the soul is given.

II

BARA HAIDD

(BARLEY BREAD)

WELSH RHYMES AND BALLADS

BARLEY BREAD

A COTTAGE on earth, and a castle in air,
And Diana Mereryd's white apron shall wear,
And bake barley bread to a tender old song
Of Love in a cottage, that always was young :
And when winter comes, and the storm holds
    the hill,
And Davyth can find no more grist for the mill,
Ah, hers are the kisses shall frighten away
The cares of his heart at the close of the day ;
When at nightfall they sit in the glow of the
    fire,
And he draws closer still as the shadows draw
    nigher ;
And the night-wind without, as it wintrily calls
From the hill to the glen, cries in window and
    walls,
Like the world's cold reply to the poet's desire.

GAENEN HIR, 1892-3.

THE MOUNTAIN COTTAGE

Far below the gold and green
High on Moel Morvyth seen,
Where more rarely thrusts the heather
Through the gorse its purple feather;
Far below, yet far aloft
From the wayward wizard Dee ;
Secret in its garden croft,
Fenced with rural mystery
By the homely mountain-sides :
There a lonely cottage hides.

There, the summer through, our cares
In the freer mountain airs
Change their guise, as may the thorn
When the wild white rose is born :
There, the early morning light,
Leading day across the height,
O'er the climbing larch-tree tops
And the birchwood's silvery copse,
Brings such greeting to our glen
And our windows, half-asleep,
That the lurking day again
Seems with sudden life to leap,

Hailed with rapturous carollings,
Lifted on a thousand wings,—
As it were the promised morn
Of the perfect day of earth,
That between his death and birth
Once for every man is born.

Now the rising sun may show
Through the treetops, all aglow,
And the lowing calf is mute,
And the blackbird drops his flute :
But the day, as you shall see,
Has a changing harmony :
Once within our threshold, all
Has its hour of festival ;
Every rafter in our rhyme
Tells of its old forest-time ;
And our lattice-windows hold
In their panes the mystic gold
Of the gorse, and many a gleam
Of the sunset's airy stream.

All too soon, the setting sun
Radiantly withdraws his light,
Solemnly, from Morvyth's height,
And the summer's day is done.

But we see the night descend
From the mountains, like a friend ;
And, if chill the twilight falls,
High we pile the fragrant hearth,
And the peace of all the earth
Settles on our lonely walls.
So we keep our evening feast
With all rural savours spread,—
Charge the cup, and break the bread,
Counting most what may seem least :
Then, if storm be all abroad,
Witching every lonely road,
And the wind cry in the tree,
And with impish hands the rain
Shake and snatch the window pane ;
Then we tell old country tales,
While without the night wind wails,
And the more, at what we hear,
Grows and glows our fireside cheer.

Many a long-gone poet, then,
In our feasting lives again :
Herrick, and old Henryson,
Milton, Marvell, Campion,
Or, the king of heart and mind,
Master of the mimic kind ;
Many more, whose names are gold,

Need not that our love be told :
Heine's note and Shelley's song
Lead us round to Burns ere long,
Or with Keats we turn and hark
His April eve of old St. Mark,
Or Wordsworth, with austerer rhyme,
Mountainous, sets thought to climb.
But of all whose hearts have sung
One there is, of older tongue,
Tunes his woodland note apart
Still more near to touch the heart :
Davyth of the leafy line
Pours for us his lyric wine,
Till our pulses thrill with song,
And all wondrous fancies throng
With an elfin melody
And a strain of old romance
Every glade and green expanse
Of the poet's forestry.

Too remote the mountain life
From the modern noise and strife,
It may seem. Yet, well it knows
Other lives and deeper throes,
Where in London's splendid dust
Men and women strive, and thrust
Weary hands to find the gold

Sunk beneath it, and grow pale,
Seeking still, that still must fail ;
While sweet youth grows keen and old,
And three times the die is cast,
Shows the master-chance is past.
Oft at night, if silence fall
In our midst, we seem to hear
London's pulse beat fast and near,
And the fierce continual call
Of its multitude that waits
A deliverer at the gates.

But another tale is ours :
All the summer history
Of the changing mountain flowers,
Of oaken bough and birchen tree ;
From the hour that sees unclose
First the shy white maiden rose,
To the empurpled August weather
When the wild-bee seeks the heather.
If our fancy, bee-like, roam,
Tired at last its wings fly home ;
As of old Glendower turned
To this vale whose name is his,
To his pastoral house of peace,
From the fields where battle burned.
Now is sheathed that ancient sword,

But its song remains, and still
Sounds from lonely field and hill,
Clear as when Glendower warred ;
Still it hangs mysteriously
On our walls, where they may see
Who have subtle art to read
All the rose in one grey seed,
All the passion of romance
In the maiden's timid glance,
All the Druids, dimly shown,
In the fallen mountain stone ;
And within our mountain gate,
All the ancient Kymric state.

Heart and harbour of our days !
If afar our feet may roam,
Glad at last we hasten home,
Following the famous ways
Where your bards and heroes passed,
Glad at heart to come at last
Here, and find a breathing space
In your mountain resting-place.

GAENEN HIR, 1892-3.

MOUNTAIN TWILIGHT

Sunset fades, and in the sky
Twilight shows that night is nigh ;
But its pale and paler glow
Lingers long on yonder stream,
Where the silent waters seem
Loth to leave the vale below.
Now the trees turn old and grey
In the wan white evening light,
While the shadows drape the day
With the purple robe of night.
Moel Morvyth's sombre height
Fills Glendower's vale with awe ;
Mountain-side, and lonely farm
Which an hour ago you saw
Nestling in the mountain's arm,
Empty road, and stream and field,
In this dusk enchantment yield
Mysteries it was not given
Even to Merlin's eye to read,
Till from earthly habit freed
On the mountain heights of heaven.

THE MOUNTAIN WEDDING

THE purple and the gold are gone
　　From Moel-y-Gamelỳn,
That made our summer crown and throne ;
And now from its cold slopes, alone
　　I watch the year close in.

The year goes fast ; now Autumn calls
　　On Winter from the hill ;
While round and round our lonely walls
The dead leaf flies and whirls and falls,
　　At wild October's will.

But these late voices of the year,
　　The dead leaf on the pane,
As love's new rhyme of love, I hear ;
They bring the bridal morning, dear,
　　When we 'll be wed again !

THE WEDDING OF PALE BRONWEN

THE wind was waked by the morning light,
  And it cried in the grey birch-tree,
And the cry was plain in Bronwen's bower,
  ' O Bronwen, come to me ! '

Pale, pale sleeps Bronwen, pale she wakes—
  ' What bird to my bower is flown ?
,For my lover, Red Ithel, is at the wars
  Before Jerusalem town.'

But still the wind cried in the tree,
  ' Come forth, 'tis your wedding morn,
And you must be wed in Holy Land
  Ere your little babe is born.'

And still the wind had her true-love's cry,
  ' Kind Bronwen, come ! ' until
She could not rest, and rose to look
  To the sea beyond Morva Hill.

And afar came the cry over Morva Hill,
  'Kind Bronwen, come to me!'
Till she could not stay, for very love,
  And stole away to the sea.

She crossed the hill to the fishing-boats,
  And away she sailed so fine,—
'Is it far, my love, in the summer sun
  To the shores of fair Palestine?'

II

There was no sun at sea that day
  To watch pale Bronwen drown;
But the sun was hot on the deadly sands
  Before Jerusalem town.

All day Red Ithel lay dying there,
  But he thought of the far-off sea;
And he cried all day till his lips grew white,
  'Kind Bronwen, come to me!'

And so it passed till the evening time,
  And then the sea-wind came,
And he thought he lay on Morva Hill
  And heard her call his name.

He heard her voice, he held her hand :
　‘ This is the day,’ she said,
‘ And this is the hour that Holy Church
　Has given, for us to wed.’

There was no strength in him to speak,
　But his eyes had yet their say,—
‘ Kind Bronwen, now we will be wed
　For ever and ever and aye ! ’

III

Beneath the sea pale Bronwen lies,
　Red Ithel beneath the sand ;
But they are one in Holy Church,
　One in love’s Holy Land.

Red Ithel lies by Jerusalem town,
　And she in the deep sea lies ;
But I trow their little babe was born
　In the gardens of Paradise.

THE HOUSE OF HENDRA

'S'ai Plas Hendre
Yn Nghaer Fyrddin :
Canu Brechfa,
Tithau Lywelyn.'

'Ef a welai hen-llys adfeiliedig, a neuadd drydoll.'

C

NOTE

Hendra'. Hendre; or Hendref: 'An old or established habitation, the same as a *ganafdy* or winter house, being opposed to the *hafotty*, or the temporary residence in the mountains, to attend the flocks during the winter months. It forms the name of many old mansions : as Hendref Gadog, Hendref Urien' (Dr. Owen Pughe). Pronounce *Haindra*. The Brechva of this poem must not be confused with the other Carmarthenshire bard of the same name.

THE HOUSE OF HENDRA

I

The House of Hendra stood in Merlin's Town, and was sung by Brechva on his Harp of gold, at the October Feasting of Ivor.

In the town where wondrous Merlin
    Lived, and still
In deep sleep, they say, lies dreaming
Near it, under Merlin's Hill.

In that town of pastoral Towy,
    Once of old
Stood the ancient House of Hendra,
Sung on Brechva's harp of gold.

With his harp to Ivor's feasting
    Brechva came,
There he sang and made this ballad,
While the last torch spent its flame.

Long they told,—the men of Ivor,
  Of the strain
At the heart of Brechva's harping,
Heard that night, and not again.

II

Incipit Brechva's Ballad of the
House of Hendra, and of his deep
sleep there on Hallowmas night,
and of his strange awaking.

In yon town, he sang,—there Hendra
  Waits my feet,
In renownéd Merlin's town where
Clare's white castle keeps the street.

There, within that house of heroes,
  I drew breath ;
And 'tis there my feet must bear me,
For the darker grace of death.

There that last year's night I journeyed,—
  Hallowmas !
When the dead of earth, unburied,
In the darkness rise and pass.

Then in Hendra (all his harp cried
  At the stroke),
Twelve moons gone, there came upon me
Sleep like death. At length I woke :

I awoke to utter darkness,
  Still and deep,
With the walls around me fallen
Of the sombre halls of sleep :

With my hall of dreams downfallen,
  Dark I lay,
Like one houseless, though about me
Hendra stood, more fast than they :

But what broke my sleep asunder,—
  Light or sound ?
There was shown no sign, where only
Night, and shadow's heart, were found.

III

Anon he hears a voice in the night,
and rising from sleep, looks out
upon the sleeping town.

So it passed, till with a troubled
  Lonely noise,
Like a cry of men benighted,
Midnight made itself a voice.

Then I rose, and from the stairloop,
  Looking down,
Nothing saw, where far before me
Lay, one darkness, all the town.

In that grave day seemed for ever
  To lie dead,
Nevermore at wake of morning
To lift up its pleasant head :

All its friendly foolish clamour,
  Its delight,
Fast asleep, or dead, beneath me,
In that black descent of night :

But anon, like fitful harping,
  Hark, a noise !
As in dream, suppose your dreamer's
Men of shadow found a voice.

IV

Hearing his name called, Brechva
descends to the postern, and sees
thence a circle of Shadows, in a
solemn dance of Death.

Night-wind never sang more strangely
  Song more strange ;
All confused, yet with a music
In confusion's interchange.

Now it cried, like harried night-birds,
  Flying near,
Now, more nigh, with multiplying
Voice on voice, 'O Brechva, hear !'

I was filled with fearful pleasure
  At the call,
And I turned, and by the stairway
Gained the postern in the wall :

Deep as Annwn lay the darkness
  At my feet ;—
Like a yawning grave before me,
When I opened, lay the street.

Dark as death, and deep as Annwn,—
  But these eyes
Yet more deeply, strangely, seeing,
From that grave saw life arise.

And therewith a mist of shadows
  In a ring,
Like the sea-mist on the sea-wind,
Waxing, waning, vanishing.

Circling as the wheel of spirits
  Whirled and spun,
Spun and whirled, to forewarn Merlin
In the woods of Caledon.

V
        The Spirits are no dream-folk ; but
        ancient inmates of the House of
        Hendra.

Shades of men, ay, bards and warriors !—
   Wrought of air,
You may deem, but 'twas no dream-folk,
Born of night, that crossed me there.

And my heart cried out,—' O Vorwyn !
   They are those
Who of old-time lived to know here
Life's great sweetness in this house.'

I had bid them kinsman's welcome,
   In a word,
For the ancient sake of Hendra,
Which they served with harp and sword.

But as still I watched them, wondering,
   Curiously,
Knowing all they should forewarn me,—
Of my death and destiny !

Ere I marked all in the silence,
   Ere I knew,
Swift as they had come, as strangely
Now their shadowy life withdrew.

The Spirits being gone, Brechva hears
aerial music, and sees in vision all the
Bards in the seventh Heaven.

They were gone ; but what sweet wonder
   Filled the air !—
With a thousand harping noises,—
Harping, chiming, crying there.

At that harping and that chiming,
   Straightway strong
Grew my heart, and in the darkness
Found great solace at that song.

Through the gate of night, its vision,
   Three times fine,
Saw the seventh heaven of heroes,
'Mid a thousand torches' shine :

All the bards and all the heroes
   Of old time
There with Arthur and with Merlin
Weave again the bardic rhyme.

There a seat is set and ready,
   And the name
There inscribed, and set on high there,—
BRECHVA of the Bards of Fame !

VII

Here ends the song with the immortal consolation of Death, and
Brechva prays for peace.

Know then, O ye men of Ivor,
  How elate
To his death at last goes Brechva,
When he fares from out your gate!

Three nights hence, and all his journeying
  Gladly done,
Then the friendly door of Hendra
Opens to her destined son.

Once more shall it open for him,
  And no more;
When they bear him out for burial,
With the singing boys before.

Then the gate of night those circling
  Spirits crossed
Shall be opened wide, and show him
Heaven and all the bardic host;

All the bards, and golden Merlin
  In the throng,
Gathered there, and harping Brechva
To his peace with solemn song.

And all peace be yours and Brechva's
   Now, and fate
In the ancient House of Hendra
Yield him soon death's high estate !

BRECHVA'S HARP SONG

'And there shall yet arise a King in Wales!'
ANCIENT PREDICTION.

LITTLE harp, at thy cry,
  He shall come in good time;
And thy sword-song on high,
  High shall chime.

Little harp, in his brain
  Is the fire; in his hand
Are the sword and the rein
  Of command.

Little harp, like the wind
  Is his strength; like thy song
Are his words, to unbind
  Wales ere long!

Little harp, if his name
  Be unknown, ye shall hear
How the stars tell his fame
  Far and near.

Little harp, if unknown
  He come, ye shall sing
When Eryri shall throne
  Him All King!

OLWEN

(from 'kilhwch and olwen')

THE message was sent, and the maiden came,
And the maiden was clad in a robe of flame,
And about her neck was a collar enrolled
Of emerald and ruby and ruddy gold.
More yellow her hair than the flower of the broom,
And her skin more white than the white sea-foam ;
And fairer her hands and her fingers fine
Than the wood-anemones that twine
In the spray of the meadow fountain's dance.
The falcon's eye, the gerhawk's glance,
Not brighter than Olwen's eyes of light ;
Her bosom was more snowy white
Than the swan's white breast, and not more red
Than Olwen's lips the roses spread :
Four white trefoils lightly leapt,
Where'er on the forest floor she stepp'd.
The forest flowers tell her fame ;
And Olwen therefore is her name.
Whoever Olwen once may see,
For ever must her lover be.

'Y FAM A'I BABAN'

(FROM THE WELSH)

THE mother yields her little babe to sleep
    Upon her tender breast,
And singing still a lullaby,
    Hushes its heart to rest:
'O sleep in peace upon my bosom,
And sweetly may your small dreams blossom:
And from the fears that made me weep you,
And from all pains, as soft you sleep you,
The angels lightly guard and keep you,
    And hold you blest!

'Your mother dear, is often full of fear,
    As the moments run;
Her love entwines so close, ah dear,
    Dearest little one.
Her song is in its music weeping,
To think of death and its dark keeping,
That yet might turn those red cheeks white,—
Life's rose, that grows so in her sight;
And your bright eyes, like morning light!—
    Dearest little one!'

THE BIRCH GROVE

(FROM DAVYTH AP GWILYM)

AH, the pleasant grove of birches,
A pleasant place to tarry all the day;
Swift green path to holiness;
Place of leaves on branches deftly strung,—
Tapestry meet for proudest princess;
Place of the thrush's voice, the king of song,
Place of the fair breasted hill, green place of tree-
    tops,
Place set apart for two, far from jealous strife;
Veil that hides the maiden at the wooing,
Full of delight is then the green birch grove.

Lo, I possess the whole extent of the birches,
Each corner of the greenwood is my throne;
I have loved as my Saviour this building of Nature,
Tapestried in tenfold royalty by the leaves of the
    grove.
The sweet-voiced nightingale beneath the green
    boughs,
Is the herald inhabitant of the wood,
Endlessly pouring his song from within the forest,

From the jutting hill and the glistening green tree-
top ;
And so I pour forth songs in praise of my green
enclosure,
My purest green parlour framed of leaves.

There is a chamber for us within the grove
Made all of young vines ;
A gleaning of the birch boughs, fair in colour,
Makes in this chamber a fragrant bed.
A place for the gentle gift of love
Is the house of leaves made by God the Father.

Fair chapel, sacred from strife,
Of boughs and leaves in the green and airy May ;
Be ye, O trees, my fitting consolation,
In that I am left houseless to-day.
O nightingale, with the grey wings trailing low,
That art from the beginning the love messenger' in
May,
Be a strong voice from the steep hillside ;
Let the day bring the meeting between Morvyth
and me !

G. R.

III

A RHYME OF DIANA

D

THE NEW DIANA

DIANA, in that older time,
　Was only a cold goddess,
Who never hid a lover's rhyme
　Within her heaving bodice.

But now, so long as love can write,
　Diana shall be human,
And to Olympian grace unite
　The sorrows of a woman.

A DREAM OF DIANA

In dream I saw Diana pass, Diana as of old,
Across the greenwood radiantly, attired in green
    and gold:
With spear alert, with eyes afire, as they had seen
    the sun,
And gave its glances back again, with brightness
    of their own;
No human maid is she, I thought, who there so
    lightly fares
Upon her sylvan empery, afar from our pale cares.

She passed, and left me to that thought, who felt
    the sadder then,
That only once, and not again, she might be seen
    of men;
Though constantly, by lawn and wood, and hanging
    mountain-side,
My restless eye might dare to hunt the huntress in
    her pride:

Without her all was lonely grown : I had no liking
    left,
For ferny glade, or fox-glove bloom, of her bright
    grace bereft.

And in that taking, in a bed of softest fern I lay,
And found no joy of woodcraft left, the livelong
    summer day ;
When lo ! at eve, a silvery horn, a questing hound,
    a cry,
And swift, Diana came again, and sat her down
    thereby :
And then I saw those radiant eyes were full of
    perfect rest,
And found beneath the goddess there, the
    woman's softer breast.

AH, DEAR DIANA

.

THIS new Diana makes weak men her prey,
  And, making captive, still would fain pursue,
And still would keep, and still would drive away,—
      So day by day,
  Hate, hunt, do murder, and yet love them too ;
           Ah, dear Diana !

'Twere well, poor fools, to shun her cruel spear,
  More fatal far than that which slew of old ;
Her spear is wit, that she so brings to bear ;
      Then laughs to hear
  When it has struck, and one more heart runs cold ;
           Ah, dear Diana !

Be wise, O fools, and shun her cruel eyes,
  Which, when you see, you straight must love, to
    death.
This new Diana has such sorceries,
      Who loves her, dies ;
  And dying, cries still, with his latest breath,—
              Ah, dear Diana !

THE MYSTICAL MOUNTAINEER

THE morning sun shone out, and showed the way,
   Showed glen and greenwood, hill and lonely height;
Said he, 'The mountains call me forth to-day':
   Said she, 'Then go; but come again to-night!'

He hailed the sun, he hailed each field and stream,
   And every hill up-poised, and every tree,
His wanderer's pulse made all the morning seem
   Some sweetest love-song's natural melody.

In glen and greenwood, hill and lonely height,
   He heard that song; whereat, as 'twere a spell
To charm the day, he saw a wondrous sight,—
   Diana everywhere: he knew her well:

He knew her well, though no one else might see
   Her by the river, and upon the height:
And as he saw, and heard that melody,
   The morning rang with the refrain, 'To-night!'

THE IDLE RHYMER

HERE alone in Aber grove
Still I match my rhymes with love,
While the good September sun
Turns the green of earth to gold,
And the river's never done
Telling secrets never told.
Here I lie, who should be bent
At my cloistral table still,
O'er the tardy instrument
Of my brain's laborious will;
Here I lie and turn to rhyme
Anything that first may rise
In my fancy's airy clime,—
Thoughts of dear Diana's eyes
When they light with wit's surprise,
(Wit, 'tis said, too quick for me,)
And their merry sudden smile,—
And the deeper mystery
Of their tears, (Here pause awhile,
While I sorrow for each tear!)

And-the beauty rare and fair
Of her form, and all the grace
Pictured in Diana's face
'Neath the halo of her hair :

Ah, ye trees of Aber glen,
If I roam apart from men,
And am idle in your grove ;
Know it is because I love,
And my rhymes absolve me then !

VI

INVOCATIONS

I

COME over, Diana, across the grey sea;
From the green hills and valleys, come over!
And bring, as you love me, the shy little key
That can open your heart to your lover!
         Come over,
            Diana, come over the sea!

II

Fair wind, blow fair, to bring Diana over!
Fair sun, shine out across the Irish sea!
And all you fragrant airs the earth sets free,
And all you lovely things, as I'm her lover,
Put on your best to bring her back to me.

NIGHT SONG

I HAVE waited long in the night for you,
  And the hour is late,
And the songs are hushed, and the watchers few,
  At the palace-gate.

The torches have lit the revellers forth, ·
  And shown them home ;
And the stars have changed in the sombre north :
  But you do not come.

The night wind stirs with a lonely sound :
  You do not know
What loneliness in my heart is found,
  As I turn to go.

PILGRIMAGE

Storm down, October, on the earth,
  As with December's rage!
Come hail or snow, I journey forth
  On lover's pilgrimage.

By field and stream, this bolder path
  I follow for her sake,
Whose thought can of the winter's wrath
  A song of summer make.

Among these wintry fells and fields,
  For her dear sake I roam,
Until some greener valley yields
  Her sweetest heart a home.

EPITHALAMION

THE pains of earth are over,
  The joys of heaven begin ;
To-night 'tis told your lover,—
  ' O wanderer, enter in !

' Her feet have passed before you,
  She opens wide the door,
Who, for the love she bore you,
  Your pain and passion bore.

' One word to your dear lady,
  And heaven is yours for aye ;
The feast is spread and ready,
  The harping minstrels play.

' Your sins of earth forgiven !
  Oh, she forgives each one ;—
Now, pilgrim, enter heaven,
  Your pilgrimage is done ! '

IV

THE ROMANCE OF JULIUS ROY

ROMANCE

HERE I must write what may never be shown you
  Till all is past—romance and its grace ;
When but the knowing how I could have known you
  Shall call up love's torchlight too late in your
    face.

Ah, starry-eyed ! shall this sorrowful passion
  But burn on out, when love is so deep ?
Why should I try then to sing, poet-fashion ?
  Far better be silent, far better asleep.

Asleep—if to dream !   No Hamlet's misgiving
  Shall e'er make me fear it.   Ah, only to dream
That we far away in some dream-land are living,
  And your eyes are alight there, the stars that
    they seem !

THE MOUNT OF VISION

' I 'll climb to-night,' he said,
' And see the day die at the feet of night,
  Till earth and heaven are back to chaos fled,
    And darkness knows not light!

' And there, as freed by death,
The world withdrawn, I 'll test the immortal fire,—
What heaven outlasts this passionate human breath,
    What love outlasts desire.'

THE DREAMER'S TRAGEDY

In the taking of dream, in the old way of sorrow,
  Led in deep sleep, through a darker than night,
Night cries I heard, unknown as the morrow,
    Crying, ' Oh see, where Saint Silvia passes!'
And I saw where she passed, like a star in the
  ⌐ height.

This is the dream that by night comes upon me,
  And leaves me to darkness more deep; for 'twas
    writ,
Writ so by fate, when her starry eyes won me:
    There is her way to the light, mine to darkness,
That's deeper dark now, for the fire she once lit.

MARGARET

THEY were two children, like these flowers,
  In changing beauty drest ;
I loved as dearly Margaret's grace
  As Silvia's deep unrest.

They were but children, and I thought,—
  I thought no harm to tell
Of the hope of eternal fame of song,
  That the poet knows so well.

But time went on, and they became
  New dowered in woman's ways,
And I saw their eyes had a deeper light
  And their forms a fairer grace,

And Silvia shone, a flower of gold,
  A flower to sun the night ;
But Margaret as the Spring's first bloom,
  That makes the sad heart light.

And light and glad, with boundless love
  My sad heart quickly grew,
And the merry sun of spring and youth
  Made all old things seem new.

And yet a little while, and then—
  And then the end was come;
And Margaret's was the way of light,
  And mine was the way of gloom.

COR MORTIS

THE way is dark and hard,
Beset by death, and darker dreams and fears ;
The way is long and dark and evil-starred ;
    And still no end appears.

With god-like challenge, life
May call me forth with sword and song to fight ;
But I go doubting, hopeless, to the strife,
    With heart of death and night.

'HAMLET' IN COUNTYTOWN

THE play was over, and to dreams consigned
  That tardy, desperate dreamer's cry of pain ;
  While through dark streets, beneath the gusty
    rain,
Now Silvia passed, and I was stayed behind
To hear the yawning critics gape their blind
  Generic commonplace, and vacant strain ;
  While Silvia passed to take the midnight train,
Smiles on her lips, old Denmark in her mind.

So much for love's delay ! A moment more,
  And then the storm stayed Silvia in the throng,—
  A moment more and she was mine at will :
In Countytown we talked of Elsinore,—
  The midnight train was grown a myth, a song,
  And the gusty climbing street, an enchanted hill.

THE MELANCHOLY JESTER

Now the end of all be sung :
He is old, who once was young ;
He is old, and to the gate
Of the gods is come too late :
Jester, gladly yield your breath ;
Now the only jest is Death.
Soon shall Silvia, passing, say—
' Faith, my clown is turned to clay :
Deep, with solemn obsequies,
Hide the clay that once was his,
Keep him, earth, sun, wind and rain,
Till his wit shall rise again ! '

THE NIGHT RIDE

To-night we rode beneath a moon
  That made the moorland pale ;
And our horses' feet kept well the tune
  And our pulses did not fail.

The moon shone clear ; the hoarfrost fell,
  The world slept, as it seemed ;
Sleep held the night, but we rode well,
  And as we rode we dreamed.

We dreamed of ghostly horse and hound,
  And flight at dead of night ;—
The more the fearful thoughts we found,
  The more was our delight.

And when we heard the white owl fly,
  And hoot with mournful tone,
We thought to see dead men go by,
  And pressed our horses on.

The merrier then was Silvia's song
  Upon the homeward road,—
Oh, whether the way be short or long
  Is all in the rider's mood !

And still our pulses kept the tale,
  Our gallop kept the tune,
As round and over hill and vale
  We rode beneath the moon.

RED ROSES, AND WHITE

RED ROSES

Roses, if my passion burn
 Red as you, with fragrant fire,
Shall it die like you, and turn
 Soon to death its great desire?

Or, shall love die every year
 But to live, with deeper hue
Every June because of her?
 Roses, shall it live like you?

No sleep like hers, no rest,
   In all the earth to-night :
Upon her whiter breast
   Our roses lie so light.

She had no sins to lose,
   As some might say ;
But calmly keeps her pale repose
   Till God's good day.

SILVIA'S SOLITUDE

She has left the places
  Of our common day;
Here are still the traces
  Where she took her way:

Here a primrose, lying
  By a beechen tree;
Here a footprint, spying
  Out her destiny.

But no tree, nor flower
  Ever in greenwood,
May lead you to the bower
  Of Silvia's solitude.

SANCTA SILVIA

She was the lady of our hearts and minds,
  Our queen of beauty, by the natural spell
  Of her deep eyes, whose hue the sky may tell;
As now it seems my fancy newly finds
Their likeness in this little brook that winds
  Reflecting every sky-change through its dell:
  So all things rare, of earth and sky, so well
Her memory keep, in all their fairest kinds.

But all her beauty had the sky's impress,
    Her eyes were tinct with : so in memory now
    An aureole of sky-born mystery plays
Above the vision of her loveliness,
    That never more on earth may make us bow
    With the old boyish chivalry of those days.

ON THE EVE

THE clouds are strangers in the sky to-night :
   Two only, far above, grey-lighted, fare
   In all the night's long wilderness of air,—
Two lonely travellers in the starry height.
Eastward, whence they are come, the sea in might
   Cries in the darkness from its wintry lair ;
   Now westward lies their way, to mountains where
Earth's ancient bastions rise against their flight.

In all the night, in mountain, sea, and sky,
   There is no augury my heart can find,
     Save in you clouds that coldly mark my fate,—
Intent to-night on pilgrimage more high,
   Barred by the ancient bastions of the mind,—
     'A journey,' say they, 'do not take !' Too
     late.

THE PRIDE OF DEATH

If adverse wind then meet my ship of fate,
  Let me be careless that thou comest, Death !
Who still would live, but know my frail estate
  To make an end full soon, and pass beneath
To thy last darkness, Death, which proudly I await.

The quondam dream that men, so passing, went
  To other seas, is gone ; with this frail breath
Ends all, I know, and sail on well content,—
  Pleased as I live with life, well pleased, O
    Death,
To meet thy wind full soon, on thy pale errand
  sent.

V
AD MATREM
AND OTHER
OCCASIONAL
VERSE

AD MATREM

There is no envied gift of perfect grace
    And priceless fragrance, but is still too poor
    To bring and lay this morning at your door
In sign of all love's quiet tale can trace,
Since first your boyish tyrants ran a race
    To hail your coming, and you still forbore
    To chide their careless hearts, that strove the
      more,
The more they read love's challenge in your face.

To riper deeds now time has called us forth,
    And wider fields, and some abroad are gone;
    But though deep seas divide, and still we roam
Unto the Indian south, or Arctic north,
    Once more to-day your love can make us one,
    And failing other gifts our love flies home.

TO WALT WHITMAN

ON HIS SEVENTIETH BIRTHDAY

HERE health we pledge you in one draught of song,
Caught in this rhymer's cup from earth's delight,
Where English fields are green the whole year long,
The wine of might,
That the new-come Spring distils, most sweet and
    strong,
In the viewless air's alembic, wrought too fine for
    sight.

Good health! we pledge, that care may lightly
    sleep,
And pain of age be gone for this one day,
As of this loving cup you take, and, drinking deep,
Grow glad at heart straightway
To feel once more the kindly heat of the sun
Creative in you, as when in youth it shone,
And pulsing brainward with the rhythmic wealth
Of all the summer whose high minstrelsy
Shall soon crown field and tree,
And call back age to youth again, and pain to
    perfect health.

May 1889.

TO PERCY

WITH A COPY OF WORDSWORTH

In the hottest crowd, when grace
Seems to hide her maiden face,
Here you 'll find a mystic voice
Full of heaven's supernal noise:
Lake and stream and woodland here
Wait you always, far, yet near;
And a breath of mountain wind
Rustling in the leaves you 'll find:
In the world's seducing clan
It shall be your talisman,—
Keep it, Percy, long in honour
Of its author (and its donor)!

TO MABEL

WITH THE 'GOLDEN TREASURY OF
SONGS AND LYRICS'

HIDDEN here, with hearts of song,
Live the poets, always young ;
Read them, Mabel, through and through ;—
They will give their hearts to you !

TO VIOLET

IN HER SICKCHAMBER

WITH SOME MOUNTAIN FLOWERS

VIOLET, we send you here
This for mountain messenger,
News from field and hill to bring
Of a day when everything
That has seemed so grey and sad
Shall again be only glad ;
When all natural things that knew you
Shall give health again unto you,
And pain's requiem be said,
And the rose be doubly red,
And all flowers in the sun
Shake their dainty frocks for fun.

Violet, the Spring is flown
When your kindred-flowers were strown
In our mountain lanes, and soon
We shall see the harvest moon :

But this mountain envoy brings
News of many other springs
Yet to come, and summer-times
Filled with finer flowers and rhymes,
When no pains of earth shall bind you,
But each sun that shines shall find you
Happier and happier yet
While your name is Violet!

TO M. H. E.

In England I know it is Spring,—
  In old England to-day,
  With primrose and violet and rare daffodil,
  In many a valley, on many a hill,
And the birds are beginning to sing,
  As I would, if I knew the way.

But I know the way of the Spring,
  When old England turns gay
  With primrose and violet and rare daffodil,
  And all that I know, you know better still,
And all that I mean, but can never sing,
  You will let my daffodils say.

Boston, U.S.A.,
  April 1888.

AT THE RHYMERS' CLUB

I. THE TOAST

SET fools untó their folly !
  Our folly is pure wit,
As 'twere the Muse turned jolly :
For poets' melancholy,—
  We will not think of it.

As once Rare Ben and Herrick
  Set older Fleet Street mad,
With wit, not esoteric,
And laughter that was lyric,
  And roystering rhymes and glad

As they, we drink defiance
  To-night to all but Rhyme,
And most of all to Science,
And all such skins of lions
  That hide the ass of time.

To-night, to rhyme as they did
　Were well,—ah, were it ours,
Who find the Muse degraded,
And changed, I fear, and faded,
　Her laurel crown and flowers.

Ah, rhymers, for that sorrow
　The more o'ertakes delight,
The more this madness borrow : —
If care be king to-morrow,
　We toast Queen Rhyme to-night.

II. MARLOWE

With wine and blood and wit and deviltry,
He sped the heroic flame of English verse :
Bethink ye, rhymers, what your claim may be,
Who in smug suburbs put the Muse to nurse ?

THE NEW KING OF BRENTFORD

TO R. LE G.

IN REMINDER OF AN OLD PROMISE [1]

Are there no buds at Brentford?
  We ask our budding rose,
Whose stem each day a tiny sword
  Of tender green, unsheathes and shows
  Against his February foes.

No cakes and ale at Brentford?—
  Though Brentford's King be dead,
We know a King whose lyric word
  Was given, in his jovial stead,
  To pour the wine, to break the bread.

---

[1] 'When there are buds enough in the garden, you two must
come and feast at Brentford!'

Are there no buds at Brentford,
　　Where, round your ancient house,
The crocus hears the blackbird
　　Bid every blade of grass arouse
　　Within the garden close?

Dear lyric King of Brentford,
　　Though March on fifty stormwinds sail,
We hold you to your royal word :
　　By every bud that feels the gale,
　　We call for cakes and ale !

A DIALOGUE

CONCERNING LOVE'S DELAYS

'Seven years Sir Song must wait for me ;
   I shall not change,'—she said.
'Seven years,' he said, 'this change may see;
   Live lords may then be dead !

'And dead may live, but live may die,
   And Love's young blood run pale ;
And year by year, ere seven go by,
   End many a true-love tale.

'Ah then, too late, your heart may say
   To Love—What, are you flown ?
When one of us is turned to clay,
   And one is worldly grown.'

THE WANTING RHYME

I would love you for ever and ever, my dear,
  And that were a little time :
I would love you for ever and ever and aye
  If your name would but rhyme.

But no rhyme can I find you, Mereryd,
  And until love find you one,
And the lover come with the wanting rhyme,
  You still must roam alone.

THE SECRET

AFTER HEINE

WE do not sigh, our eyes are tearless;
And if we smile, we laugh no more;
Never shall the hidden secret
From our eyes gleam as of yore.

The ancient wound, for ever aching,
Throbs on beneath its blood-red stain;
Within the heart its pang is hidden,
Within the lips its speechless pain.

Ask of the babe within the cradle,
Ask of the dead within the grave:
'Tis only these can ever tell you,
What fate as secret to me gave.

WALES England wed ; so I was bred. 'Twas merry
London gave me breath.
I dreamt of love, and fame : I strove. But Ireland
taught me love was best :
And Irish eyes, and London cries, and streams of
Wales, may tell the rest.
What more than these I asked of Life, I am
content to have from Death.

G

THE LAST WORD

THE last word 's uttered, and the last line writ,
　　Of thought's long tarrying in these quiet walls ;
　　And now oppressively the feeling falls
That all the past, by hope and wonder lit,
May never more renew the noble heat
　　And passionate hope of youth, that set the blood
　　So wildly brainward, as it surely would
Have throbbed aloud, and made men know of it.

But what has been may never be again ;
　　Even now to-morrow dawns, another day,
　　　Whose sun is not the sun that shone before
And painted Heaven on my window pane :
　　To-morrow comes, and points the different way,
　　　That I must take, and so return no more.

THE MOUNTAIN SONG

A FABLE FOR CRITICS, BY WAY OF EPILOGUE

Now came Diana, as in ancient story,
    With shining spear, and tunic gold and green,
      And I, of late so sorry,
Grew glad again to see her, the forest boughs
    between.

'What news?' I cried: 'A-hunting I have
    been,
    To find the fawn,' she said, 'and took this bird,
      Whose like I have not seen!'
Within her hand I saw then, where some silver
    feathers stirred.

Her hand she opened, and a note we heard,
    And ruffling wings, and straight, away it flew ;—
      Yet not as if it feared,
But as if it needs must haste to the mountain
    haunts it knew.

And piping as it passed, its silvery hue
    Gleaming afar, like sun on April grass,
      We heard it still pursue
Its piping way and disappear within the moun-
    tain pass.

But much I wondered what wild kind it was,
    And asked Diana, what its forest name?
      She laughed—she said, 'Because
I fear its unknown note foretells your doubtful
    fame.

' For few will understand, and many blame,
    The simple piping of your unknown song,
      And many cry you shame;
And yet your rhyme shall turn again, and keep
    its mountain tongue.

' And if it fail, it shall not be for long:
    For some there are who knew the note before;
      And some who did you wrong
Shall find that piping in their ears, and lose the
    spell no more!'

List of Books

in

Belles Lettres

ALL BOOKS IN THIS CATALOGUE
ARE PUBLISHED AT NET PRICES

1894

Telegraphic Address—
'BODLEIAN, LONDON'

'A WORD must be said for the manner in which the publishers have produced the volume (*i.e.* "The Earth Fiend"), a sumptuous folio, printed by CONSTABLE, the etchings on Japanese paper by MR. GOULDING. The volume should add not only to MR. STRANG'S fame but to that of MESSRS. ELKIN MATHEWS AND JOHN LANE, who are rapidly gaining distinction for their beautiful editions of belles-lettres.'—*Daily Chronicle*, Sept. 24, 1892.

Referring to MR. LE GALLIENNE'S 'English Poems' *and* 'Silhouettes' by MR. ARTHUR SYMONS :—'We only refer to them now to note a fact which they illustrate, and which we have been observing of late, namely, the recovery to a certain extent of good taste in the matter of printing and binding books. These two books, which are turned out by MESSRS. ELKIN MATHEWS AND JOHN LANE, are models of artistic publishing, and yet they are simplicity itself. The books with their excellent printing and their very simplicity make a harmony which is satisfying to the artistic sense.'—*Sunday Sun*, Oct. 2, 1892.

'MR. LE GALLIENNE is a fortunate young gentleman. I don't know by what legerdemain he and his publishers work, but here, in an age as stony to poetry as the ages of Chatterton and Richard Savage, we find the full edition of his book sold before publication. How is it done, MESSRS. ELKIN MATHEWS AND JOHN LANE? for, without depreciating MR. LE GALLIENNE'S sweetness and charm, I doubt that the marvel would have been wrought under another publisher. These publishers, indeed, produce books so delightfully that it must give an added pleasure to the hoarding of first editions.'—KATHARINE TYNAN in *The Irish Daily Independent*.

'To MESSRS. ELKIN MATHEWS AND JOHN LANE almost more than to any other, we take it, are the thanks of the grateful singer especially due; for it is they who have managed, by means of limited editions and charming workmanship, to impress book-buyers with the belief that a volume may have an æsthetic and commercial value. They have made it possible to speculate in the latest discovered poet, as in a new company—with the difference that an operation in the former can be done with three half-crowns.'
St. James's Gazette.

List of Books

IN

BELLES LETTRES

(*Including some Transfers*)

PUBLISHED BY

Elkin Mathews and John Lane

𝕮𝖍𝖊 𝕭𝖔𝖉𝖑𝖊𝖞 𝕳𝖊𝖆𝖉

VIGO STREET, LONDON, W.

N.B.—The Authors and Publishers reserve the right of reprinting any book in this list if a second edition is called for, except in cases where a stipulation has been made to the contrary, and of printing a separate edition of any of the books for America irrespective of the numbers to which the English editions are limited. The numbers mentioned do not include the copies sent for review or to the public libraries.

ADAMS (FRANCIS).
    ESSAYS IN MODERNITY. Cr. 8vo. 5s. net. [*Immediately.*

ALLEN (GRANT).
    THE LOWER SLOPES: A Volume of Verse. 600 copies.
        Cr. 8vo. 5s. net.

ANTÆUS.
    THE BACKSLIDER AND OTHER POEMS. 100 only.
        Small 4to. 7s. 6d. net. [*Very few remain.*

BENSON (EUGENE).
    FROM THE ASOLAN HILLS: A Poem. 300 copies. Imp.
        16mo. 5s. net. [*Very few remain.*

BINYON (LAURENCE).
>   LYRIC POEMS.   With Title-page by SELWYN IMAGE.
>   Sq. 16mo.   5s. net.

BOURDILLON (F. W.).
>   A LOST GOD : A Poem.   With Illustrations by H. J. FORD.
>   500 copies.   8vo.   6s. net.   [*Very few remain.*

CHAPMAN (ELIZABETH RACHEL).
>   A LITTLE CHILD'S WREATH : A Sonnet Sequence.
>   350 copies.   Sq. 16mo.   3s. 6d. net.

COLERIDGE (HON. STEPHEN).
>   THE SANCTITY OF CONFESSION : A Romance.   Second
>   Edition.   Crown 8vo.   3s. net.   [*A few remain.*

CRANE (WALTER).
>   RENASCENCE : A Book of Verse.   Frontispiece and 38
>   designs by the Author.
>   [*Small paper edition out of print.*
>   There remain a few large paper copies, fcap. 4to. £1, 1s. net.
>   And a few fcap. 4to, Japanese vellum. £1, 15s. net.

CROSSING (WM.).
>   THE ANCIENT CROSSES OF DARTMOOR.   With 11 plates.
>   8vo, cloth.   4s. 6d. net.   [*Very few remain.*

DAVIDSON (JOHN).
>   PLAYS : An Unhistorical Pastoral ; A Romantic Farce ;
>   Bruce, a Chronicle Play ; Smith, a Tragic Farce ;
>   Scaramouch in Naxos, a Pantomime, with a Frontis-
>   piece, Title-page, and Cover Design by AUBREY
>   BEARDSLEY.   500 copies.   Small 4to.   7s. 6d. net.

DAVIDSON (JOHN).
>   FLEET STREET ECLOGUES.   Second Edition.   Fcap. 8vo,
>   buckram.   5s. net.

DAVIDSON (JOHN).
>   A RANDOM ITINERARY : Prose Sketches, with a Ballad.
>   Frontispiece, Title-page, and Cover Design by LAUR-
>   ENCE HOUSMAN.   Fcap. 8vo.   Uniform with 'Fleet
>   Street Eclogues.'   5s. net.

DAVIDSON (JOHN).

THE NORTH WALL. Fcap. 8vo. 2s. 6d. net.
The few remaining copies transferred by the Author to the present Publishers.

DE GRUCHY (AUGUSTA).

UNDER THE HAWTHORN, AND OTHER VERSES. Frontispiece by WALTER CRANE. 300 copies. Crown 8vo. 5s. net. [*Very few remain.*
Also 30 copies on Japanese vellum. 15s. net.

DE TABLEY (LORD).

POEMS, DRAMATIC AND LYRICAL. By JOHN LEICESTER WARREN (Lord De Tabley). Illustrations and Cover Design by C. S. RICKETTS. Second Edition. Crown 8vo. 7s. 6d. net.

FIELD (MICHAEL).

SIGHT AND SONG. (Poems on Pictures.) 400 copies. Fcap. 8vo. 5s. net. [*Very few remain.*

FIELD (MICHAEL).

STEPHANIA: A Trialogue in Three Acts. 250 copies. Pott 4to. 6s. net. [*Very few remain.*

GALE (NORMAN).

ORCHARD SONGS. Fcap. 8vo. With Title-page and Cover Design by J. ILLINGWORTH KAY. 5s. net.
Also a Special Edition limited in number on hand-made paper bound in English vellum. £1, 1s. net.

GARNETT (RICHARD).

POEMS. With Title-page designed by J. ILLINGWORTH KAY. 350 copies. Crown 8vo. 5s. net.

GOSSE (EDMUND).

THE LETTERS OF THOMAS LOVELL BEDDOES. Now first edited. Pott 8vo. 5s. net.

GRAHAME (KENNETH).

PAGAN PAPERS: A Volume of Essays. With Title-page by AUBREY BEARDSLEY. Fcap. 8vo. 5s. net.

GREENE (G. A.).

> ITALIAN LYRISTS OF TO-DAY. Translations in the original metres from about thirty-five living Italian poets, with bibliographical and biographical notes. Crown 8vo. 5s. net.

HAKE (DR. T. GORDON).

> A SELECTION FROM HIS POEMS. Edited by Mrs. MEYNELL. With a Portrait after D. G. ROSSETTI, and a Cover Design by GLEESON WHITE. Crown 8vo. 5s. net.

HALLAM (ARTHUR HENRY).

> THE POEMS, together with his essay 'On Some of the Characteristics of Modern Poetry and on the Lyrical Poems of ALFRED TENNYSON.' Edited, with an Introduction, by RICHARD LE GALLIENNE. 550 copies. Fcap. 8vo. 5s. net.   [*Very few remain.*

HAMILTON (COL. IAN).

> THE BALLAD OF HADJI AND OTHER POEMS. Etched Frontispiece by WM. STRANG. 50 copies. Fcap. 8vo. 3s. net.
>
> *Transferred by the Author to the present Publishers.*

HAZLITT (WILLIAM).

> LIBER AMORIS, a reprint of the 1823 edition, with numerous original documents appended never before printed, including Mrs. Hazlitt's Diary in Scotland, Portrait after Bewick, Facsimile Letters, etc., and the Critical Introduction by RICHARD LE GALLIENNE prefixed to the edition of 1893. A limited number only. 4to. £1, 1s. net.   [*In the Press.*

HICKEY (EMILY H.).

> VERSE TALES, LYRICS AND TRANSLATIONS. 300 copies. Imp. 16mo. 5s. net.

HORNE (HERBERT P.).
DIVERSI COLORES : Poems. With ornaments by the
Author. 250 copies. 16mo. 5s. net.

JAMES (W. P.).
ROMANTIC PROFESSIONS : A Volume of Essays, with Title-
page by J. ILLINGWORTH KAY. Crown 8vo. 5s. net.

JOHNSON (EFFIE).
IN THE FIRE AND OTHER FANCIES. Frontispiece by
WALTER CRANE. 500 copies. Imp. 16mo. 3s. 6d.
net.

JOHNSON (LIONEL).
THE ART OF THOMAS HARDY : Six Essays. With
Etched Portrait by WM. STRANG, and Bibliography
by JOHN LANE. Crown 8vo. 5s. 6d. net.
Also 150 copies, large paper, with proofs of the portrait. £1, 1s.
net. [*Very shortly.*

JOHNSON (LIONEL).
A VOLUME OF POEMS. Fcap. 8vo. 5s. net.
[*In preparation.*

KEATS (JOHN).
THREE ESSAYS, now issued in book form for the first time.
Edited by H. BUXTON FORMAN. With Life-mask
by HAYDON. Fcap. 4to. 10s. 6d. net.
[*Very few remain.*

KEYNOTES SERIES.
Each volume complete in itself. Crown 8vo, cloth.
3s. 6d. net.
Vol. I. KEYNOTES. By GEORGE EGERTON. With
Title-page by AUBREY BEARDSLEY.
[*Fourth edition now ready.*
Vol. II. POOR FOLK. Translated from the Russian of
F. Dostoievsky by LENA MILMAN. With
a Preface by GEORGE MOORE.
[*In rapid preparation.*

KEYNOTES SERIES—*continued.*

Vol. III. THE DANCING FAUN. By FLORENCE EMERY.

Vol. IV. A CHILD OF THE AGE. By FRANCIS ADAMS.
[*Shortly.*]

Vol. V. THE GREAT GOD PAN AND THE INMOST LIGHT. By ARTHUR MACHEN.
[*Shortly.*]

LEATHER (R. K.).

VERSES. 250 copies. Fcap. 8vo. 3s. net.
Transferred by the Author to the present Publishers.

LEATHER (R. K.), & RICHARD LE GALLIENNE.

THE STUDENT AND THE BODY-SNATCHER AND OTHER TRIFLES. [*Small paper edition out of print.*]
There remain a very few of the 50 large paper copies. 7s. 6d. net.

LE GALLIENNE (RICHARD).

PROSE FANCIES. With a Portrait of the Author by WILSON STEER. Crown 8vo. Purple cloth, uniform with 'The Religion of a Literary Man.' 5s. net.
Also a limited large paper edition. 12s. 6d. net.

LE GALLIENNE (RICHARD).

THE BOOK BILLS OF NARCISSUS. An Account rendered by RICHARD LE GALLIENNE. Second Edition. Crown 8vo, buckram. 3s. 6d. net.

LE GALLIENNE (RICHARD).

ENGLISH POEMS. Third Edition, crown 8vo. Purple cloth, uniform with 'The Religion of a Literary Man.' 5s. net.

LE GALLIENNE (RICHARD).

GEORGE MEREDITH: Some Characteristics. With a Bibliography (much enlarged) by JOHN LANE, portrait, etc. Third Edition. Crown 8vo. 5s. 6d. net.

LE GALLIENNE (RICHARD).
THE RELIGION OF A LITERARY MAN. 3rd thousand.
Crown 8vo. Purple cloth. 3s. 6d. net.
Also a special rubricated edition on hand-made paper. 8vo.
10s. 6d. net.

LETTERS TO LIVING ARTISTS.
500 copies. Fcap. 8vo. 3s. 6d. net. [*Very few remain.*

MARSTON (PHILIP BOURKE).
A LAST HARVEST: LYRICS AND SONNETS FROM THE
BOOK OF LOVE. Edited by LOUISE CHANDLER
MOULTON. 500 copies. Fcap. 8vo. 5s. nèt.
Also 50 copies on large paper, hand-made. 10s. 6d. net.
[*Very few remain.*

MARTIN (W. WILSEY).
QUATRAINS, LIFE'S MYSTERY AND OTHER POEMS. 16mo.
2s. 6d. net. [*Very few remain.*

MARZIALS (THEO.).
THE GALLERY OF PIGEONS AND OTHER POEMS. Fcap.
8vo. 4s. 6d. net. [*Very few remain.*
Transferred by the Author to the present Publishers.

MEYNELL (MRS.), (ALICE C. THOMPSON).
POEMS. Second Edition. Fcap. 8vo. 3s. 6d. net. A
few of the 50 large paper copies (First Edition) remain.
12s. 6d. net.

MEYNELL (MRS.).
THE RHYTHM OF LIFE, AND OTHER ESSAYS. Second
Edition. Fcap. 8vo. 3s. 6d. net. A few of the 50
large paper copies (First Edition) remain. 12s. 6d. net.

MONKHOUSE (ALLAN).
BOOKS AND PLAYS: A Volume of Essays. 400 copies.
Crown 8vo. 5s. net.

MURRAY (ALMA).
PORTRAIT AS BEATRICE CENCI. With critical notice
containing four letters from ROBERT BROWNING.
8vo, wrapper. 2s. net.

NETTLESHIP (J. T.).
    ROBERT BROWNING : Essays and Thoughts.   A Third
        Edition is in preparation.   Crown 8vo.   5s. 6d. net.
        Half a dozen of the Whatman large paper copies
        (First Edition) remain.   £1, 1s. net.

NOBLE (JAS. ASHCROFT).
    THE SONNET IN ENGLAND AND OTHER ESSAYS.   Title-
        page and Cover Design by AUSTIN YOUNG.   600
        copies.   Crown 8vo.   5s. net.
        Also 50 copies large paper.   12s. 6d. net.

NOEL (HON. RODEN).
    POOR PEOPLE'S CHRISTMAS.   250 copies.   16mo.   1s. net.
                                    [*Very few remain.*

OXFORD CHARACTERS.
    A series of lithographed portraits by WILL ROTHENSTEIN,
        with text by F. YORK POWELL and others.   To be
        issued monthly in term.   Each number will contain
        two portraits.   Parts I. to V. ready.   200 sets only,
        folio, wrapper, 5s. net per part; 25 special large
        paper sets containing proof impressions of the por-
        traits signed by the artist, 10s. 6d. net per part.

PINKERTON (PERCY).
    GALEAZZO : A Venetian Episode and other Poems.
        Etched Frontispiece.   16mo.   5s. net.
                                 [*Very few remain.*
    Transferred by the Author to the present Publishers.

RADFORD (DOLLIE).
    SONGS.   A New Volume of Verse.   [*In preparation.*

RADFORD (ERNEST).
    CHAMBERS TWAIN.   Frontispiece by WALTER CRANE.
        250 copies.   Imp. 16mo.   5s. net.
        Also 50 copies large paper.   10s. 6d. net.   [*Very few remain.*

RHYS (ERNEST).
    A LONDON ROSE AND OTHER RHYMES.   With Title-page
        designed by SELWYN IMAGE.   500 copies.   Crown
        8vo.   5s. net.

RICKETTS (C. S.) AND C. H. SHANNON.

HERO AND LEANDER. By CHRISTOPHER MARLOWE and GEORGE CHAPMAN. With Borders, Initials, and Illustrations designed and engraved on the wood by C. S. RICKETTS and C. H. SHANNON. Bound in English vellum and gold. 200 copies only. 35s. net.

RHYMERS' CLUB, THE BOOK OF THE.

A second volume will appear in the Spring of 1894.

SCHAFF (DR. P.).

LITERATURE AND POETRY: Papers on Dante, etc. Portrait and Plates, 100 copies only. 8vo. 10s. net.

STODDARD (R. H.).

THE LION'S CUB; WITH OTHER VERSE. Portrait. 100 copies only, bound in an illuminated Persian design. Fcap. 8vo. 5s. net. *[Very few remain.*

STREET (G. S.).

THE AUTOBIOGRAPHY OF A BOY. Passages selected by his friend G. S. S. With Title-page designed by C. W. FURSE. 500 copies. Fcap. 8vo. 3s. 6d. net.

SYMONDS (JOHN ADDINGTON).

IN THE KEY OF BLUE, AND OTHER PROSE ESSAYS. Cover designed by C. S. RICKETTS. Second Edition. Thick Crown 8vo. 8s. 6d. net.

THOMPSON (FRANCIS).

POEMS. With Frontispiece, Title-page and Cover Design by LAURENCE HOUSMAN. Fourth Edition. Pott 4to. 5s. net.

TODHUNTER (JOHN).

A SICILIAN IDYLL. Frontispiece by WALTER CRANE. 250 copies. Imp. 16mo. 5s. net. Also 50 copies large paper, fcap. 4to. 10s. 6d. net. *[Very few remain.*

TOMSON (GRAHAM R.).
> AFTER SUNSET. A Volume of Poems. With Title-page and
> Cover Design by R. ANNING BELL. Fcap. 8vo. 5s.
> net.
>
> Also a limited large paper edition. 12s. 6d. net. [*In preparation.*

TREE (H. BEERBOHM).
> THE IMAGINATIVE FACULTY : A Lecture delivered at the
> Royal Institution. With portrait of Mr. TREE from
> an unpublished drawing by the Marchioness of Granby.
> Fcap. 8vo, boards. 2s. 6d. net.

TYNAN HINKSON (KATHARINE).
> CUCKOO SONGS. With Title-page and Cover Design by
> LAURENCE HOUSMAN. 500 copies. Fcap. 8vo. 5s.
> net.

VAN DYKE (HENRY).
> THE POETRY OF TENNYSON. Third Edition, enlarged.
> Crown 8vo. 5s. 6d. net.
>
> *The late Laureate himself gave valuable aid in correcting*
> *various details.*

WATSON (WILLIAM).
> THE ELOPING ANGELS: A Caprice. Second Edition.
> Square 16mo, buckram. 3s. 6d. net.

WATSON (WILLIAM).
> EXCURSIONS IN CRITICISM : being some Prose Recrea-
> tions of a Rhymer. Second Edition. Cr. 8vo. 5s. net.

WATSON (WILLIAM).
> THE PRINCE'S QUEST, AND OTHER POEMS. With a
> Bibliographical Note added. Second Edition. Fcap.
> 8vo. 4s. 6d. net.

WEDMORE (FREDERICK).
> PASTORALS OF FRANCE—RENUNCIATIONS. A volume of
> Stories. Title-page by JOHN FULLEYLOVE, R.I.
> Third Edition. Crown 8vo. 5s. net.
>
> *A few of the large paper copies of Renunciations (First Edition)*
> *remain.* 10s. 6d. net.

WICKSTEED (P. H.).
DANTE. Six Sermons. Third Edition. Crown 8vo. 2s. net.

WILDE (OSCAR).
THE SPHINX. A poem decorated throughout in line and
colour, and bound in a design by CHARLES RICKETTS.
250 copies. £2, 2s. net. 25 copies large paper.
£5, 5s. net.

WILDE (OSCAR).
The incomparable and ingenious history of Mr. W. H.,
being the true secret of Shakespear's sonnets now for
the first time here fully set forth, with initial letters
and cover design by CHARLES RICKETTS. 500 copies.
10s. 6d. net.
Also 50 copies large paper. 21s. net.   [*In preparation.*

WILDE (OSCAR).
DRAMATIC WORKS, now printed for the first time with a
specially designed Title-page and binding to each
volume, by CHARLES SHANNON. 500 copies. Small
4to. 7s. 6d. net per vol.
Also 50 copies large paper. 15s. net per vol.
Vol. I. LADY WINDERMERE'S FAN : A Comedy in
Four Acts.   [*Ready.*
Vol. II. A WOMAN OF NO IMPORTANCE : A Comedy
in Four Acts.   [*Shortly.*
Vol. III. THE DUCHESS OF PADUA : A Blank Verse
Tragedy in Five Acts.   [*In preparation.*

WILDE (OSCAR).
SALOMÉ : A Tragedy in one Act, done into English.
With 11 Illustrations, Title-page, and Cover Design
by AUBREY BEARDSLEY. 500 copies. Small 4to.
15s. net.
Also 100 copies, large paper. 30s. net.

WYNNE (FRANCES).
WHISPER. A Volume of Verse. With a Memoir by
Katharine Tynan and a Portrait added. Fcap. 8vo.
2s. 6d. net.
Transferred by the Author to the present Publishers.

The Hobby Horse

A new series of this illustrated magazine will be published quarterly by subscription, under the Editorship of Herbert P. Horne. Subscription £1 per annum, post free, for the four numbers. Quarto, printed on hand-made paper, and issued in a limited edition to subscribers only. The Magazine will contain articles upon Literature, Music, Painting, Sculpture, Architecture, and the Decorative Arts; Poems; Essays; Fiction; original Designs; with reproductions of pictures and drawings by the old masters and contemporary artists. There will be a new title-page and ornaments designed by the Editor. Among the contributors to the Hobby Horse are :

The late MATTHEW ARNOLD.
LAURENCE BINYON.
WILFRID BLUNT.
FORD MADOX BROWN.
The late ARTHUR BURGESS.
E. BURNE-JONES, A.R.A.
AUSTIN DOBSON.
RICHARD GARNETT, LL.D.
A. J. HIPKINS, F.S.A.
SELWYN IMAGE.
LIONEL JOHNSON.
RICHARD LE GALLIENNE.
SIR F. LEIGHTON, Bart., P.R.A.
T. HOPE MCLACHLAN.
MAY MORRIS.
C. HUBERT H. PARRY, Mus. Doc.
A. W. POLLARD.

F. YORK POWELL.
CHRISTINA G. ROSSETTI.
W. M. ROSSETTI.
JOHN RUSKIN, D.C.L., LL.D.
FREDERICK SANDYS.
The late W. BELL SCOTT.
FREDERICK J. SHIELDS.
J. H. SHORTHOUSE.
The late JAMES SMETHAM.
SIMEON SOLOMON.
A. SOMERVELL.
The late J. ADDINGTON SYMONDS.
KATHARINE TYNAN.
G. F. WATTS, R.A.
FREDERICK WEDMORE.
OSCAR WILDE.

Prospectuses on Application.

THE BODLEY HEAD, VIGO STREET, LONDON, W.

'Nearly every book put out by Messrs. Elkin Mathews &
John Lane, at the Sign of the Bodley Head, is a satisfaction to
the special senses of the modern bookman for bindings, shapes,
types, and papers.   They have surpassed themselves, and
registered a real achievement in English bookmaking by the
volume of " Poems, Dramatic and Lyrical," of Lord De Tabley.'
Newcastle Daily Chronicle.

'A ray of hopefulness is stealing again into English poetry
after the twilight greys of Clough and Arnold and Tennyson.
Even unbelief wears braver colours.   Despite the jeremiads,
which are the dirges of the elder gods, England is still a nest
of singing-birds (*teste* the Catalogue of Elkin Mathews and John
Lane).'—Mr. ZANGWILL in *Pall Mall Magazine.*

'All Messrs. Mathews & Lane's Books are so beautifully
printed and so tastefully issued, that it rejoices the heart of a
book-lover to handle them ; but they have shown their sound
judgment not less markedly in the literary quality of their
publications.   The choiceness of form is not inappropriate to
the matter, which is always of something more than ephemeral
worth.   This was a distinction on which the better publishers
at one time prided themselves ; they never lent their names to
trash ; but some names associated with worthy traditions have
proved more than once a delusion and a snare.   The record of
Messrs. Elkin Mathews & John Lane is perfect in this respect,
and their imprint is a guarantee of the worth of what they
publish.'—*Birmingham Daily Post*, Nov. 6, 1893.

'One can nearly always be certain when one sees on the title-
page of any given book the name of Messrs Elkin Mathews &
John Lane as being the publishers thereof that there will be
something worth reading to be found between the boards.'—
World.

Edinburgh: T. and A. CONSTABLE
Printers to Her Majesty